Finding the Glory of God in the Face of Jesus Christ

JanMarie Holzberger

ISBN: 979-8-9952096-0-7

All Scripture is taken from the open domain (King James) Version.

https://thegrowingchristian.com

TABLE OF CONTENTS

PREFACE

2 Corinthians 4:6

For God, who commanded the light to shine out of darkness, hath shined in our hearts, to give the light of the knowledge of the glory of God in the face of Jesus Christ.

This lesson utilizes the teachings of the prophets, apostles, and the teachings of Jesus to reveal who Jesus is and how to obey His command in Matthew 28:19. This simple lesson allows us to see the connections between the writings of the prophets, the Words of Jesus, and the writings of the apostles in an enlightening way.

Ephesians 2:19-21

Now therefore ye are no more strangers and foreigners, but fellow citizens with the saints, and of the household of God; [20]And are built upon the foundation of the apostles and prophets, Jesus Christ himself being the chief corner stone; [21]In whom all the building fitly framed together groweth unto an holy temple in the Lord:

TEACHERS GUIDE

As a visual learner, I don't always absorb what I read. Diagrams and charts help me understand the topic. Having taught for over 30 years, including homeschooling my own six children, I know people have different learning styles. Like me, they learn best by seeing pictures or diagrams to add context to what they read or hear.

As a teacher, I wanted a Bible study that would engage people across all learning styles. I asked the Lord to help me create a lesson on finding His glory in Jesus Christ that would use all the learning gates. This booklet is the product of that prayer. To Jesus belongs all the glory and the honor.

This booklet can be used as a teacher's guide or for personal growth. The verses are meant to be read aloud so the eyes see, and the ears hear. Each student is encouraged to create their own chart or diagram of the verses, so the hand writes it. Note pages are provided so that other reference Scriptures and thoughts can be added.

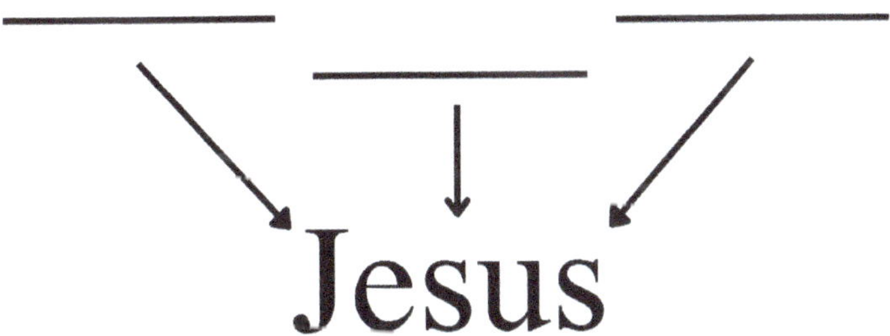

It is my prayer that this Bible Study is used to bless the believers of Jesus Christ and be a catalyst for transformation in their lives.

THE CORNERSTONE OF DOCTRINE

The cornerstone is the foundational part on which something's existence, stability, success, or truth depends. Our faith is to be built on the foundation of the apostles and prophets, with Jesus Christ being the fundamental part on which our existence and success depend. Since Jesus is the truth and the way to eternal life, we need to know as much as possible about Him. Our study starts in the Old Testament with the writing of the prophet Isaiah.

Every year at the celebration of Jesus' birth, a verse of Scripture appears on Christmas cards around the world.

Isaiah 9:6
For unto us a child is born, unto us a son is given: and the government shall be upon his shoulder: and his name shall be called Wonderful, Counsellor, The mighty God, The everlasting Father, The Prince of Peace.

This Scripture appears on Christmas cards every year because scholars agree that the verse refers to Jesus Christ.

I'd like to draw your attention to some key insights about Jesus in this passage. Isaiah 9:6 reveals that Jesus is the mighty God and the everlasting Father.

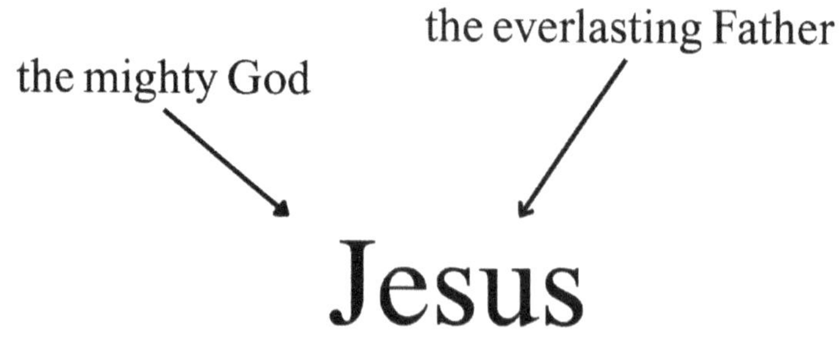

Turning to the New Testament, let's look at Mark 1:1

Mark 1:1
The beginning of the gospel of Jesus Christ, the Son of God;

This verse says Jesus is the Son of God.

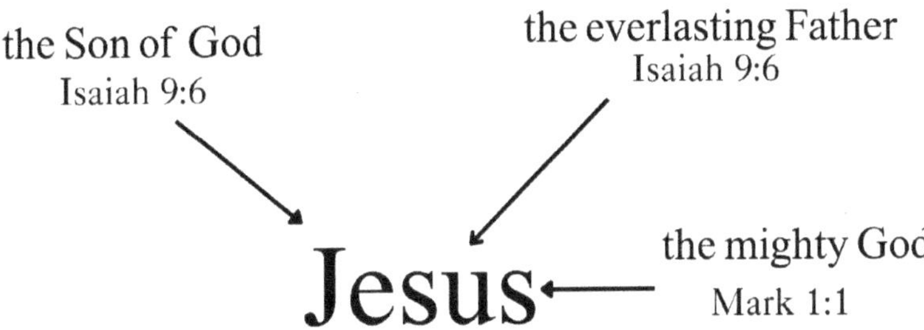

Turning to the words of Jesus Himself, let's look at John 14:26.

John 14:26
But the Comforter, which is the Holy Ghost, whom the Father will send in my name, he shall teach you all things, and bring all things to your remembrance, whatsoever I have said unto you.

Other versions of the Bible refer to the Holy Ghost as the Holy Spirit. From this point, I will use the modern term Holy Spirit instead of Holy Ghost.

The Holy Ghost/Spirit is sent in Jesus' name.

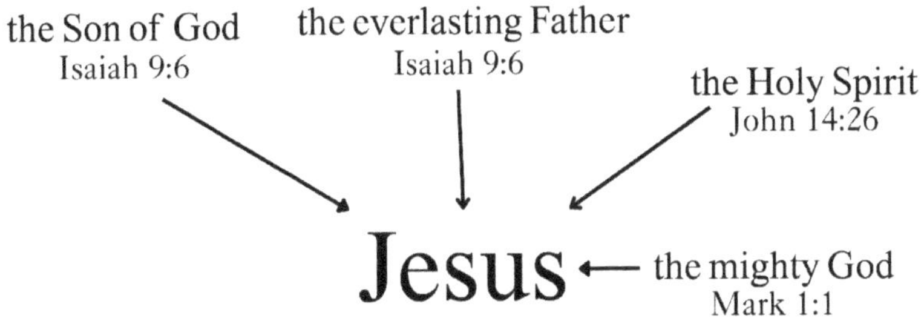

NOTES

THE ATTRIBUTES OF JESUS

Proverbs 25:2
It is the glory of God to conceal a thing: but the honour of kings is to search out a matter.

It is our privilege and honor to search out the truth presented in Scripture. Jesus often taught in ways that only genuine truth seekers would understand. With that in mind, let's take a closer look at John chapter 14, where Jesus reveals something significant about Himself.

John 14:6
Jesus saith unto him, I am the way, the truth, and the life: no man cometh unto the Father, but by me.

The Truth

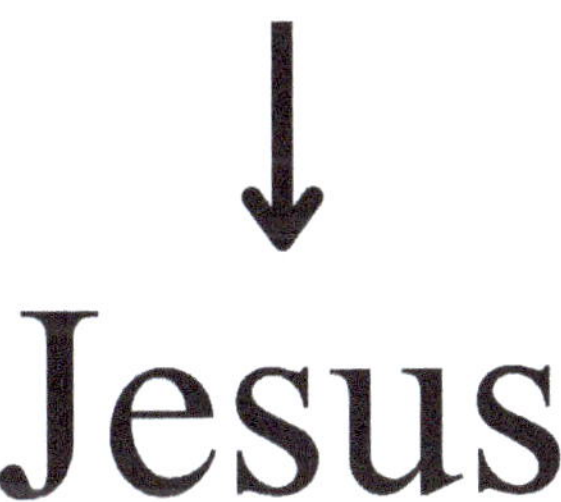

John 14:16-17
And I will pray the Father, and he shall give you another Comforter, that he may abide with you for ever; [17]Even the Spirit of truth; whom the world cannot receive, because it seeth him not, neither knoweth him: but ye know him; for he dwelleth with you, and shall be in you.

In John 14:6, Jesus says, "I am the truth." In this verse, He tells His disciples that the Comforter is the Spirit of truth. Jesus is the truth, so the Comforter is the Spirit of Jesus. This fits the rest of the verse. Jesus referred to the Spirit of truth as "Him" and said they know Him because He lives with them and later will live in them. At this point, Jesus had been living with them for almost three and a half years.

John 14:26
But the Comforter, which is the Holy Ghost, whom the Father will send in my name, he shall teach you all things, and bring all things to your remembrance, whatsoever I have said unto you.

The Comforter = the Holy Spirit. The Holy Spirit is sent in Jesus' name because the Holy Spirit is the Spirit of Jesus.

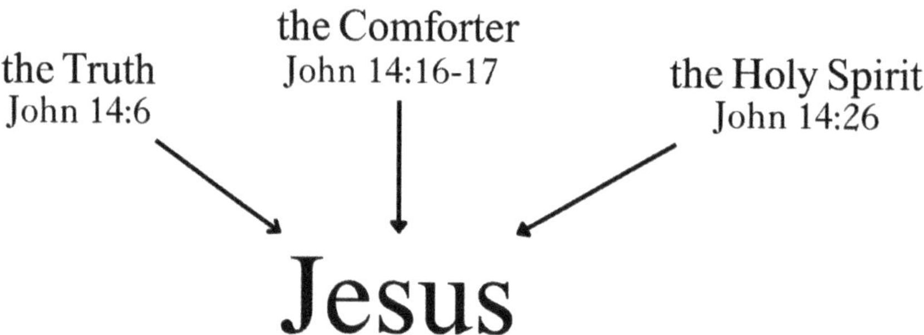

Galatians 4:6
And because ye are sons, God hath sent forth the Spirit of his Son into your hearts, crying, Abba, Father.

The Holy Spirit is the Spirit of Jesus
… and He will be in us.

NOTES

DISCOVERING HIS GLORY

Throughout John 14, Jesus is unpacking who He is to His disciples. His disciples were focused on the flesh or the natural man. Jesus - in the flesh - was the Son of God. (He now has a glorified body.) But Jesus revealed to them that He was more than the Son of God.

John 14:8
Philip saith unto him, Lord, shew us the Father, and it sufficeth us.

Jesus, hearing this question, seemed incredulous at His lack of understanding.

John 14:9
Jesus saith unto him, Have I been so long time with you, and yet hast thou not known me, Philip? he that hath seen me hath seen the Father; and how sayest thou then, Shew us the Father?

John 14:11
Believe me that I am in the Father, and the Father in me: or else believe me for the very works' sake.

The Father was in Jesus. Jesus was in the Father. Jesus put it this way.

John 10:30
I and my Father are one."

1 John 5:7
For there are three that bear record in heaven, the Father, the Word, and the Holy Ghost: and these three are one.

From John 1:14, Jesus is the Word made flesh.

John 1:14
And the Word was made flesh, and dwelt among us, (and we beheld his glory, the glory as of the only begotten of the Father,) full of grace and truth.

The Father, Jesus, and the Holy Spirit are one. This leads us back to our diagram. We really can find the glory of God in the face of Jesus Christ.

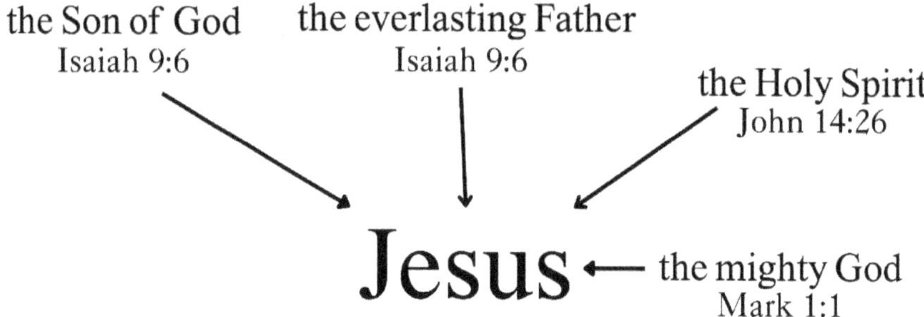

FINDING THE GLORY IN HIS COMMANDMENTS

2 Corinthians 4:6
For God, who commanded the light to shine out of darkness, hath shined in our hearts, to give the light of the knowledge of the glory of God in the face of Jesus Christ.

The best way to follow Jesus' commands is to examine how His Apostles fulfilled them.

Ephesians 2:19-21
Now therefore ye are no more strangers and foreigners, but fellow citizens with the saints, and of the household of God; [20]And are built upon the foundation of the apostles and prophets, Jesus Christ himself being the chief corner stone; [21]In whom all the building fitly framed together groweth unto an holy temple in the Lord:

The Apostles laid the foundation for us, teaching Jesus as the chief cornerstone. The cornerstone is the essential part on which something's existence, stability, success, or truth depends. With this in mind, let's determine how the Apostles obeyed Jesus' command in Matthew 28:19.

Matthew 28:19
Go ye therefore, and teach all nations, baptizing them in the name of the Father, and of the Son, and of the Holy Ghost:

Jesus gave the command. The question is: How did the Apostles obey His command? What did they teach, preach, and live by?

NOTES

THE NAME OF JESUS

Since Father, Son, and Holy Spirit are titles, we are left with the question, "What is the name?"

Proverbs 30:4
Who hath ascended up into heaven, or descended? who hath gathered the wind in his fists? who hath bound the waters in a garment? who hath established all the ends of the earth? what is his name, and what is his son's name, if thou canst tell?

It is almost as if the writer is taunting and provoking us into searching out the name. Our God, who inspired the writer of this verse, knew that understanding the name would be essential to our obedience to Jesus' command in Matthew 28:19. Since Jesus said, "… in the name of …"

Jesus said, "... in the name." He references that one name by using the titles of the name bearer. If the titles were the names, He would have said, '… in the names of…'

There is only one name. That one name is the name of the Father, the Son, and the Holy Spirit.

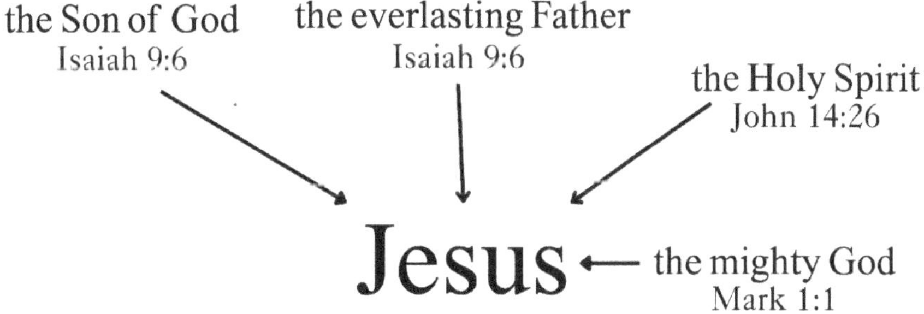

Acts 2:38
Then Peter said unto them, Repent, and be baptized every one of you in the name of Jesus Christ for the remission of sins, and ye shall receive the gift of the Holy Ghost.

I have heard it said, "I would rather obey Jesus than Peter." They were referring to the fact that Jesus said to baptize in the name of the Father, and of the Son, and of the Holy Spirit. The Apostle Peter taught the people to be baptized in the name of Jesus Christ. People who say this demonstrate a common lack of understanding.

Baptizing with the titles of Father, Son, and Holy Spirit or Holy Ghost is a widespread tradition in many churches. Just because it is tradition does not make it correct.

We can have confidence in the Apostles' teaching because the Holy Bible provides many verses to support it.

Luke 24:44-45
And he said unto them, These are the words which I spake unto you, while I was yet with you, that all things must be fulfilled, which were written in the law of Moses, and in the prophets, and in the psalms, concerning me.
45 Then opened he their understanding, that they might understand the scriptures,

Jesus personally gave them the understanding of the Scriptures.

Luke 24:46-47

And said unto them, Thus it is written, and thus it behoved Christ to suffer, and to rise from the dead the third day: [47]And that repentance and remission of sins should be preached in his name among all nations, beginning at Jerusalem.

Jesus told them to preach repentance and the remission of sins in His name, and to start in Jerusalem. The remission of sins only takes place in the waters of baptism. Peter obeyed this command on the day of Pentecost in Jerusalem. Did Peter make a mistake?

Matthew 16:16-19

And Simon Peter answered and said, Thou art the Christ, the Son of the living God. [17]And Jesus answered and said unto him, Blessed art thou, Simon Barjona: for flesh and blood hath not revealed it unto thee, but my Father which is in heaven. [18]And I say also unto thee, That thou art Peter, and upon this rock I will build my church; and the gates of hell shall not prevail against it. [19]And I will give unto thee the keys of the kingdom of heaven: and whatsoever thou shalt bind on earth shall be bound in heaven: and whatsoever thou shalt loose on earth shall be loosed in heaven.

Jesus gave Peter the keys to the Kingdom of Heaven and told him, "Whatever you loose on earth will be loosed in heaven." Peter preached the doctrine of Acts 2:38, unlocking the way to a relationship with God. He released that doctrine on earth, and it is backed by heaven.

Jesus did not contradict Himself by commanding the Apostles to preach repentance and remission of sins in His name and then commanding them to baptize in the name of the Father, and of the Son, and of the Holy Spirit. He knew that there is only one name that remits sins, and that remission of sins happens in the water of baptism in His name.

NOTES

JESUS IS THE ANSWER

The answer to the question in Proverbs 30:4 is Jesus. Jesus is the name of the Father, of the Son, and of the Holy Spirit. His disciples understood the name to be Jesus. Peter and the other eleven apostles were not disobedient to Jesus' commands. In the anointing of the Holy Spirit, Peter stood up on the day of Pentecost in Jerusalem and preached how to fulfill the command Jesus gave in Matthew 28:19.

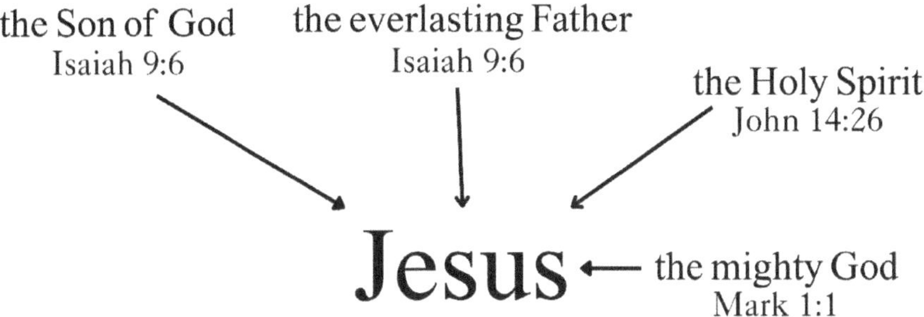

Matthew 28:19
Go ye therefore, and teach all nations, baptizing them in the name of the Father, and of the Son, and of the Holy Ghost: - Jesus commanded

Acts 2:38`
Then Peter said unto them, Repent, and be baptized every one of you in the name of Jesus Christ for the remission of sins, and ye shall receive the gift of the Holy Ghost. - Peter obeyed.

The Apostles and disciples practiced what they preached.

PRACTICING WHAT THEY PREACHED

Acts 8:14-17

Now when the apostles which were at Jerusalem heard that Samaria had received the word of God, they sent unto them Peter and John: [15]Who, when they were come down, prayed for them, that they might receive the Holy Ghost: [16](For as yet he was fallen upon none of them: only they were baptized in the name of the Lord Jesus.) [17]Then laid they their hands on them, and they received the Holy Ghost.

The disciples of Jesus Christ, Philip, Peter, and John, were trained by the Master. Jesus taught them, gave them understanding, and ordained them to go forth and preach the truth. What did they teach about baptism? How did they baptize the people? In the verses above, Philip baptized in the name of the Lord Jesus.

Acts 10:44-48

While Peter yet spake these words, the Holy Ghost fell on all them which heard the word. [45]And they of the circumcision which believed were astonished, as many as came with Peter, because that on the Gentiles also was poured out the gift of the Holy Ghost. [46]For they heard them speak with tongues, and magnify God. Then answered Peter, [47]Can any man forbid water, that these should not be baptized, which have received the Holy Ghost as well as we? [48]And he commanded them to be baptized in the name of the Lord. Then prayed they him to tarry certain days.

Here in Acts 10, Peter commanded the people to be baptized in the name of the Lord. What is the name of the Lord? His name is Jesus.

Paul was also taught by Jesus Christ by direct revelation.

Galatians 1:11-12
But I certify you, brethren, that the gospel which was preached of me is not after man. [12]For I neither received it of man, neither was I taught it, but by the revelation of Jesus Christ.

What did he teach and practice concerning water baptism?

Acts 19:1-7
And it came to pass, that, while Apollos was at Corinth, Paul having passed through the upper coasts came to Ephesus: and finding certain disciples,
[2]He said unto them, Have ye received the Holy Ghost since ye believed? And they said unto him, We have not so much as heard whether there be any Holy Ghost. [3]And he said unto them, Unto what then were ye
baptized? And they said, Unto John's baptism. [4]Then said Paul, John verily baptized with the baptism of repentance, saying unto the people, that they should believe on him which should come after him, that is, on Christ
Jesus. [5]When they heard this, they were baptized in the name of the Lord
Jesus. [6]And when Paul had laid his hands upon them, the Holy Ghost came
on them; and they spake with tongues, and prophesied. [7]And all the men were about twelve.

He also commanded the people to be baptized in the name of the Lord Jesus.

We have to ask ourselves, "Why are these accounts included in the Bible?" We know from Scripture that all Scripture is given by the inspiration of God. He has a purpose for every word recorded for us in the Holy Bible. These accounts are included as a testimony to us and as a clear example of how to practice what Jesus commanded.

It now becomes an issue of obedience. Entrance to the kingdom of heaven is only through Jesus Christ. Those who were baptized into John's baptism needed to be rebaptized in the name of Jesus Christ, the Lord.

If our baptism was in the titles Father, Son, and Holy Spirit or Holy Ghost, we have followed a widespread and long-standing church tradition but have not fulfilled what Jesus commanded in Matthew 28:19 or what Peter preached in Acts 2:38.

Each of us needs to know what was proclaimed over us during our baptism. The power to remit sins is in the spoken name of Jesus Christ, not in the titles. If you do not know what was spoken over you in baptism, or realize you were baptized in the titles of God and not the name of Jesus, I encourage you to get rebaptized in the name of Jesus Christ. You will join the many in the Bible and in churches around the world who updated their baptism when confronted with a more perfect understanding of the Word of God.

Knowing the name of God carries importance in water baptism. God also gives many promises to those who know His name. Let's look at a few of those.

Psalms 9:10
And they that know thy name will put their trust in thee: for thou, Lord, hast not forsaken them that seek thee.

Psalms 91:14
Because he hath set his love upon me, therefore will I deliver him: I will set him on high, because he hath known my name.

Paul gave us a strong warning.

Colossians 2:8-10
Beware lest any man spoil you through philosophy and vain deceit, after the tradition of men, after the rudiments of the world, and not after Christ. [9]For in him dwelleth all the fulness of the Godhead bodily. [10]And ye are complete in him, which is the head of all principality and power:

In the body of Jesus Christ dwelt the fullness of God - Father, Son, and Holy Spirit. As our diagram shows, we can truly find the glory of God in the face of Jesus Christ.

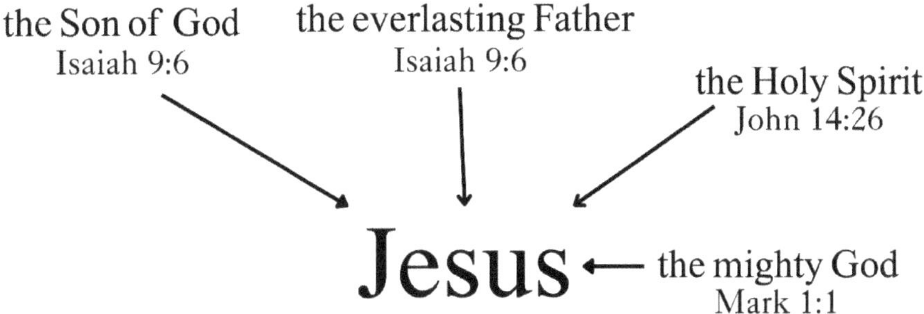

In conclusion,

1 Timothy 3:16
And without controversy great is the mystery of godliness: God was manifest in the flesh, justified in the Spirit, seen of angels, preached unto the Gentiles, believed on in the world, received up into glory.

NOTES

NOTES

ACKNOWLEDGEMENTS

All praise and Glory to Jesus Christ

Scripture quotations taken from the Authorized (King James) Version. Rights in the Authorized Version in the United Kingdom are vested in the Crown. Reproduced by permission of the Crown's patentee, Cambridge University Press.

Book design, layout and formatting by Rachel Holzberger.

The Growing Christian website https://thegrowingchristian.com has video devotionals on this and many other topics concerning our walk with God. As well as links to its podcast, social media.

AUTHOR BIOGRAPHY

In 1989, I received the gift of the Holy Spirit and had my sins washed away in the powerful name of Jesus Christ. I was born again. My husband, Bill, and all six of our children have also been born again and are faithfully serving Jesus Christ. All my children, sons-in-law, grandchildren, and husband are a constant source of inspiration and blessing to me.

My teaching journey began where I worked as a training manager and continued once I became a Christian. Shortly after my conversion, I started teaching Sunday school. This experience taught me so much about sharing His Word. In 2006, I earned my bachelor's degree in Ministerial Studies. It took me some time to achieve this goal, as I was homeschooling six children, managing my household, and serving in my local church's children's ministry.

One evening in 2020, I sat down at the table to pray. During this time of prayer, God instructed me to establish a ministry called "The Growing Christian" (TGC). His message was clear: "Make the Word of God simple so that everyone can grow in Me." This mandate guides everything I strive to create, including Bible study materials, booklets, videos, podcasts, and blogs. God's Word is not complicated; it is straightforward yet rich, profound, and layered with meaning.

I remember many church services when my heart soared during the preaching. However, I struggled to apply what was taught to my walk with Jesus. As a visual learner, I found it difficult to connect the spoken messages to my personal faith journey. I often felt that the practical application of the teachings eluded me. As I have grown older and gained more experience with Jesus, my familiarity with His Word has deepened. I feel a strong calling from the Lord Jesus to simplify this process so that people can grow quickly in their relationship with Him.

www.ingramcontent.com/pod-product-compliance
Lightning Source LLC
LaVergne TN
LVHW021131160826
845679LV00015B/1714
* 9 7 9 8 9 9 5 2 0 9 6 0 7 *